# The Ultimat
## Guide to Bu
### Dru

## Hunter Mays

# Table of Contents

4. Introduction

6. Types of Drugs

22. Cost

24. Where to Go and What to Ask For

29. Staying Safe

32. A Couple of War Stories

38. Conclusion

# INTRODUCTION

So you want to buy some drugs? Are you absolutely sure? I don't know if you've heard, but they're not always good for you. You already knew that? Okay then, I just wanted to make sure. After all, even though the government, police, your boss and your mum might not agree, the choice of whether or not to alter the makeup of your brain - using any of the vast range of narcotics, psychotropics, pharmaceuticals, stimulants, tranquilisers, plant extracts and synthetic chemicals that can be found on the black market – is YOUR CHOICE and yours alone. If you're still in, then here's a little bit of guidance from an experienced space traveller, on some useful approaches and strategies for navigating the drug world.

Oh yes, young mind-hopper, what you are about to read is the real deal. The straight dope on the world of dope; authentic advice on intoxicants and the weird and wild people that come with them. And this advice comes straight from the horse's mouth, the "horse" in this case being a hardened brain-abuser who has managed to gather together the scattered remnants of his faculties for just long enough to pass on the benefits of his experiences, dubious though those benefits may be. I'm about to tell you about all sorts of exotic chemicals, speaking from experience and a working knowledge both of their delicious effects and the damage they can cause. It goes without saying that all names have been changed.

# TYPES OF DRUGS

Assuming that you're starting from a position of relative ignorance on this subject, it might make sense to start by describing some of the substances that are out there, in terms of the types, appearance and effects, as well as some of the terminology that surrounds them. Let's get specific.

## *MARIJUANA

Eldest and greatest of all the drugs, this plant has been used by humans for as long as our kind has walked the earth, to expand consciousness, aid contemplation, achieve detachment, and generally make the daily grind a little easier to bear. It's available in a wide variety of forms, ranging from the basic plant itself to different processed versions. All of these go by a variety of different names, depending on where you are. A good catch-all term is "ganja", which is used quite universally to refer to any kind of weed. "Cannabis" is the more official term used in the English speaking world.

The basic plant is known as "bush weed" in the UK, or "schwag" in the US. Generally, it's a darkish green colour, and tends to have a high content of seeds which should be removed before smoking. Bush weed is a relatively mild product, that often comes from places such as Thailand or Jamaica, where it's grown outdoors in large quantities. It's good for a relaxed kind of smoking, where you don't get too intoxicated quickly and can go about your day with a gentle buzz on.

Other, more potent varieties of ganja are also available. Skunk is a more powerful version of the cannabis plant. It's usually grown in more of a controlled, intensive way, with small scale cultivation of crops that often involves specialised equipment such as hydroponics. As such, it's much more expensive by weight. A massive range of strains of skunk appear on the market, ranging from basic stuff to high-end, luxury brands. Skunk generally gets you much more stoned than weed does, with some strains offering a very high concentration of THC (one of the main active cannabinoid ingredients, which creates the stoned effect in your brain.) A lot of people find skunk a bit much, and avoid it in favour of gentler forms of weed. On the other hand, many hardened skunk heads won't touch anything else. Personally, I used to smoke skunk on a daily basis but nowadays give it a wide berth. It's worth mentioning that the majority of cannabis related illnesses, such as schizophrenia, psychosis and so on, can be attributed to heavy skunk consumption. On the other hand, many people smoke skunk regularly for years on end without suffering any apparent ill effects. It's up to you to maintain awareness of your own unique mind and body, and to know your own limits.

The other main category of ganja is hashish, or hash for short. Whereas skunk and bush weed are both essentially dried plant matter, hash has a rather different appearance and smell – it comes in solid pieces that resemble stone or brick, of colours ranging from brown to grey to black, depending on type. Hash is made by extracting the sap, crystal or powder from the ganja plant, and processing these extracts into a solid form. Broadly speaking, hashes are divided into two types, depending on which type of plant extract is used as the base. Powder hashes are a lighter brown or grey colour, and have a sandy, crumbly texture. In the UK, this type of hash is known as "pollen", which comes from the Dutch "pollem." Sap hashes are a darker brown to black colour, and have a stickier texture that bears some resemblance to plasticine.

In many parts of the world, such as most African and many Asian countries, bush weed is mainly what's available if you're looking for ganja. Skunk is found mostly in the western world, and is widespread throughout Western Europe and the US. It's often referred to as "chronic" in North America.

Consuming ganja is done mostly by smoking it, although it can also be eaten, either straight or by preparing it with other ingredients in a more palatable form. For the most part, cooking with ganja involves preparing "cannabutter" by frying it in butter or oil, and then using the resultant mixture in baked recipes. You could do it more simply, by just sprinkling ganja over your food. Smoking ganja can be done through a variety of means. One of the most popular of these is rolling a joint, also known as a "spliff", "zoot", "bifter" or "booder", amongst other names. A joint is basically a hand-rolled marijuana cigarette, made using rolling paper and your ganja, either pure or mixed with tobacco. Joint rolling technique is a rich subject in itself, and skill in this area can win a real craftsman lots of praise. Beyond the basic form of the joint, some virtuosos can produce huge and complex structures that defy belief. At a birthday party of mine years ago, we went around the whole party with a begging bowl, and dozens of people put in a spliff's worth each of their ganja. With the proceeds, my friend Jack rolled a joint that was the height of a small child; a gigantic, conical structure that needed two pairs of hands to hold it steady as it was smoked. It went around the whole party several times, and was appreciated and applauded by all.

Otherwise, a great variety of pipes and pipe-like devices exist for ganja smoking. These range from glass-blown pipes (prevalent in the US) to the chillums of India, to bongs (water pipes) and more extreme bong variations such as "buckets" and "lungs", designed to fill your chest with the largest volume of smoke in the quickest time possible.

Ganja can be a wonderful thing. The key is to moderate your use, and not let it get on top of you. Use it to enhance your experiences, not limit them. It can be an aid to contemplation and meditation, but it can easily work in the opposite direction, facilitating nothing more than torpor and increasing dependence on TV and junk food. Smoke ganja wisely.

*ECSTASY

After marijuana, the most commonly used street drug (in most of the English-speaking world, anyway) is ecstasy. This ultimate party drug used to be taken in the form of pills, but nowadays it's more often found in powdered crystal form. The active substance in ecstasy is MDMA, so this powder's street name is "mandy" (or "molly" in some parts of the US). It's taken by swallowing, or snorting after crushing it fine, and its effect is an intense feeling of elation and love for your fellow man. It's a wonderful drug for a number of different situations – you can dance all night with no abatement of energy at a live music event, but it's also great to just spend time with a small group of people and talk for hours on end. Ecstasy gives an increased sense of empathy, so you'll confess your innermost secrets and form bonds that can last in the long term.

Like any drug, abuse of ecstasy can have awful results. Because it works by making your brain release its store of "happy chemicals" such as serotonin, over-use of Ecstasy over a long period of time can lead to long-term psychological damage.

## *COCAINE

Cocaine is a pretty widespread drug across much of the western world. It's a white powder, consumed by snorting through the nostrils. In its pure form, cocaine is a distilled extract of the coca plant. This plant is native to South America, and indeed high quality cocaine is available quite cheaply in countries such as Peru and Colombia. However, in Europe and the US this drug is much more expensive, and tends to be used by those who have money to burn, as part of a flash, high-cost lifestyle. Cocaine is a stimulant, or "upper", and creates a sense of heightened well-being and energy. However, it doesn't bring with it the same empathy that Ecstasy does. Whereas the archetypal Ecstasy user is on a real love trip and wants to talk and listen for hours, a cocaine user tends to be on more of an ego trip, and just loves the sound of their own voice.

Crack is a more toxic and dangerous derivative of cocaine. It takes the form of small "rocks" which are smoked in pipes. It goes without saying that it's highly addictive and damaging.

*PSYCHEDELICS

The psychedelic category of drugs refers to those substances which affect your mind in a way that's different from just stimulating or tranquilising you, Instead, psychedelics have a more profound effect on the mind. There are many different psychedelic drugs, each with their own effect, that also differs widely from person to person. The best overall description that I can give is that they take you out of yourself; perhaps the best psychedelic trip of all is when the mental boundary between yourself and the rest of the universe is temporarily erased, and you perceive all of life as a single entity, manifesting itself in a plethora of earthly forms merely as a matter of detail. Whether this seems like an appealing prospect to you, or seems like absolute nonsense, it is a transcendental experience, which has a lot in common with the higher perceptions which can be reached through spiritual practices such as meditation. On the other hand, a negative psychedelic experience, or "bad trip", can leave you trembling with terror and existential despair, as the darkest elements of your consciousness are ripped open and you are subjected to hours of torment by your personal demons.

In the above descriptions, I've tried to put into words two extremes at either end of the psychedelic spectrum. Not all psychedelic trips are this intense! You might just as well pass an enjoyable afternoon on a mild trip, giggling at the flowers in a sunny meadow. It is fair to say, though, that psychedelics are generally a more serious undertaking than smoking a spliff or taking a pill, and indeed a lot of negative experiences happen when people take them without being fully aware of what they are getting into.

A wide variety of psychedelic drugs exist. Some are fairly widespread, whereas finding others requires gaining access to a small inner circle of dedicated psychedelic explorers. One reasonably commonplace psychedelic substance is psilocybin, which is the active chemical in what are known as "magic mushrooms", or "shrooms" for short. These psychedelic fungi grow naturally across much of northern Europe and elsewhere, and people pick them in large numbers in rural areas during the right season. This does require accurate knowledge of the mushrooms in question, as many different species grow in the wild. Otherwise, shrooms can generally be purchased at the right time of the year. You could even take the route of growing them yourself, by cultivating the right spores in damp, dark conditions. Anyway, shrooms are generally taken in either fresh or dried form, with the dried form obviously being much more potent by weight. They can just be eaten straight, or prepared into foodstuffs to make them more palatable. Dried shrooms can be made into tea, or even smoked. The effect of shrooms differs widely, depending on the species and other factors. Some shrooms have a visually hallucinogenic effect, so you can enjoy watching inanimate objects dancing around, and the features on your friends' faces morphing and changing. Others have an effect that is more internal and reflective.

LSD, or "acid", is a famous psychedelic drug, with a rich cultural history rooted in the 60s subculture. Good acid is still on the market today, but be careful; a variety of dodgy chemicals are peddled under the catch-all name of "acid" by some unscrupulous vendors. The LSD chemical itself is extremely potent, and doses are measured in micrograms. A typical single dose is 100 micrograms. In my experience, the effect of acid is less on the senses, and more on your consciousness at a root or base level. I've never really seen crazy stuff that isn't there on acid, but I have hugged trees, spent hours staring at insects in the grass and even had out of body experiences.

Another strong psychedelic is salvia divinorum. This potent herb has a history of use in ancient druidic ceremonies and the like. Until recently, salvia was legal in the UK, and freely available in some shops. However, the legislation against legal highs has put paid to that. It used to be possible to buy salvia extract, of varying strength. This extract would be smoked in a bong or a pipe, and send the user on a wild hallucinogenic journey. Although the effect actually lasts only a few minutes, it feels like an eternity while you're on it. On salvia, you leave reality altogether, and return back to where you were, feeling rather confused and disoriented.

DMT is a pretty crazy psychedelic drug. Popular lore has it that DMT is released by the human brain in large amounts at the point of death, so in fact taking DMT is like the experience of death itself, synthesised into a smokeable drug. Whether this is true or not is impossible to determine; but for sure the DMT trip is a mind-blowing one, that turns your mind inside out and pulls the rug out from under the parameters of your existence.

Nowadays, a wide variety of psychedelics are also available which have been synthesised in laboratories. One such set of drugs is the 2C group, which are compounds of an active drug related to mescaline, and inactive halogens. Thus, once 2CI was made illegal, 2CI, with the same effect but technically a different chemical, became available.

*KETAMINE

Originally a pharmaceutical tranquiliser used in veterinary treatment, ketamine is a drug that is now widely used on a recreational basis. That's right, humans now shovel this rotten stuff, developed to knock out horses, up their noses. It takes the form of a white powder, which can be formed into lines and snorted. Ketamine works both as a downer and a psychedelic. Its effect is dissociative, which means that taking it makes your mind much less aware of your body and its surroundings. As you take more, your ability to speak and control your limbs is reduced. Your eyes glaze over and you find it increasingly difficult to stand up, let alone engage with the outside world in any meaningful way. Inside your mind, though, the carnival really gets going. It's very difficult to put the ketamine trip into words. In small doses, it just makes everything nicely blurry and can even be energising in a strange way. However, there's a critical mass of ketamine consumption, and when you go deep enough to cross this line then you enter what's known as the "K-hole." This really is an alternate reality, which can be pretty scary but also exhilarating. It's a surreal dream world, where your consciousness is turned inside out and gradually reconstructed.

Unfortunately, ketamine is highly addictive, and this addiction can be hugely damaging to the body in quite a short time, with disastrous effects on the kidneys and bladder. The last ten years or so, when ketamine has been widely available throughout Europe and the US, have seen a large number of cases of young people suffering permanent damage to their health as a result of habitual ketamine use. However, moderate and careful use of ketamine, if you can manage this, is an enjoyable way to waste time.

# *OPIATES

The class of opiates refers to the set of drugs that are based on the opium plant. These range from a fairly raw, unprocessed version of the plant extract, all the way to medical drugs that feature the active chemicals of opium as active ingredients. These include morphine, which is still the main painkiller used in hospitals in serious cases. The effects of opiates are tranquilising and soporific; users generally don't move much, and feel calm, safe and free from worry.

Heroin is another derivative of morphine. As is well known, heroin is highly addictive and destructive. In the drug taking world, it's generally seen as the worst drug of all, with many people avoiding it like the plague even as they embrace other dangerous drugs. It's either smoked or injected, and people become addicted very quickly, going on to lose control of their lives and becoming slaves to their habit. Heroin isn't really a recreational drug, and you'll avoid it if you know what's good for you.

This is by no means a complete list of street drugs, but it covers a large proportion of what's generally available.

# COST

Prices of drugs do vary widely, generally depending on where you are and who you know. Of course, what you get when you buy drugs also differs a lot. With marijuana, for example, you can buy it really cheaply in places where it grows easily and not regulated too much, such as many African and Asian countries. You might pay the local equivalent of a couple of dollars and get enough marijuana to smoke for several days, but it would probably be pretty basic "bush weed.", the simple and unprocessed form of the plant. On the other hand, you might pay ten times as much for a lower weight of marijuana in a European country or the US, but you would probably get a stronger and more professional product. In the south of England, the cost of marijuana is increased noticeably in the last couple of years, and you generally have to pay upwards of 20 pounds($25) for just a couple of grams. Cocaine typically costs around 50 pounds($66) for a gram, or even more for high-grade or purer product. MDMA comes at around 40 pounds($53) a gram. Ketamine was as little as 15 pounds($20) a gram just a couple of years ago, but following a big drought (lack of supply) prices have now gone up to as much as 30 or 40 pounds per gram($40-$53).

It should be stated again that prices really do differ massively, according to location as well as other factors, and it's not really possible to give a useful guide to pricing, as any such set of figures is completely based in one location and one point in time. While market rates do exist for different drugs in different areas, they are very prone to change over time, as well as fluctuating hugely from place to place.

If you're lucky, you might be able to cultivate a relationship with a supplier where they will give you discounts, or "mates' rates" – supplying you with drugs at a lower cost to that charged to the average customer. This tends to apply in the case of a pre-existing friendship between dealer and customer, rather than when the relationship begins in these terms.

# WHERE TO GO AND WHAT TO ASK FOR

The drug world is a vast network of connections. Like any other product, its supply chain connects the producers to the importers, all the way through to the wholesalers and the retailers. Of course, the clandestine and underground nature of these particular products means that you can't just go to a high store shop and pick them up. Instead, being able to pick up drugs generally depends on meeting the right people. The whole thing operates very much on a word-by-mouth basis.

To be fair in most big cities, it is possible to find shady characters who hang around on street corners and sell drugs to random members of the public. They will usually be found in the hip, creative areas or the run-down parts, as opposed to the business districts. However, if you make a purchase from one of these people, you do run the strong risk of getting ripped off; you'r e likely to end up with low-quality drugs, low weights, or even total nonsense like grams of soap powder or pieces of wood that look like hash.

Drug dealers can also often be found circulating at events such as music festivals, where they can do a brisk trade selling their wares to a receptive audience. Obviously, I'm referring to some types of event rather than others; you'll find dealers at festivals featuring music such as rock, dance and reggae, rather than at those with a line-up of choral ensembles and classical orchestras. Certainly at festivals such as Glastonbury, Sziget and Burning Man, dealers make their rounds, often roaming the campsite areas calling attention to their products in much the same way as market traders do. You're less likely to get totally ripped off by one of these guys than by some nefarious character on the street, but you still probably won't get the best bang for your buck.

In my opinion, you're much better off finding a drug dealer who comes recommended by someone you know. If you think you don't know anyone with such underworld connections, you might well be mistaken. Cast your mind around your circle of friends and acquaintances, and in all likelihood there are at least one or two people who might give a cheeky grin and make a phone call for you, if you ask them at the right point. New to a city and don't know too many people? You'd do well to somehow get yourself to a place where young people congregate, such as a house party, or a club night. Sidle up to some likely-looking characters, make eye contact, and quite simply ask if they know where you can get any weed, or pills, or coke, as it might be. You'll have to overcome any shyness you feel about this, as well as the possibility of getting a frosty reception from several people before you meet the right one who will help you out.

Sooner or later, you'll meet a bona fide dealer, whose business it is to provide consumers such as yourself with the substances they're looking for. Ideally, you'll find a reliable one who provides a good service, and can supply you with a decent product at a fair price. If you can get a recommendation from someone who speaks highly of that dealer, that's the best situation – it's best to deal with friends of friends if possible.

Dealers can be a funny bunch, who have often been made quite paranoid by the combination of their trafficking of illegal substances, and their own use of these substances. Be aware that dealers tend to have their own practices regarding how they do business. One guy will travel across town to drop off a small amount at your home, another will expect you to come pick it up from them even if you want a larger amount, whereas a few people insist on meeting outside in out of the way places, back alleys and the like. It's best not to push against these requirements, as they usually represent iron clad rules that the dealer has made for themselves, whether this seems rational or not. If you don't like their rules, then unfortunately there's not much you can do about it until you have the option of going to another dealer instead.

Another thing to be aware of is to avoid mentioning any specifics or names of drugs over the phone. Dealers tend to be a bit paranoid about this, and it's best just to call them and ask if you can meet, rather than saying what you want explicitly on the phone or by text message. Some people use code words or phrases to refer to things, which has always seemed a bit silly to me. However, this practice is quite widespread, particularly amongst younger dealers, and the general rule again applies: if you want a particular dealer to supply you, you'll have to follow their requirements.

Nowadays I hear that lots of the kids are ordering their drugs online, through the Dark Net and such, which I suppose is a more convenient way of doing things, but to me takes away a lot of the excitement and adventure of the whole thing. I'm a rather old school character; I've never ordered drugs online, and wouldn't really be able to give advice on how to go about doing so. When I was living in London, though, a neighbour did mention once that they'd gone online, just using Google, and succeeded in getting marijuana delivered to their flat via courier; apparently this is a service that exists, and might well be worth trying out.

# STAYING SAFE

Obviously, it's very important to maintain a level of secrecy around any involvement with drugs. You need to ensure that your acquisition and use of drugs, and your intoxication thereof, are not apparent to the powers that be – police, your boss, the nightclub bouncer, and so on. If you're using drugs in a small way, i.e. just occasionally and in small amounts, this shouldn't really be too difficult, and is largely a matter of common sense. Be careful about where you consume drugs. If you're in a private residence, the risk is minimal, though you should be aware that the fragrance of burning ganja does travel, so you might want to avoid smoking within smelling distance of nosy neighbours.

If you're smoking or sniffing substances in a public place, such as a nightclub or on the street, you have to take much more care. Watch out if you've got drugs in your pocket while moving around a big city, as police do patrol areas such as train stations and busy shopping centres, sometimes with sniffer dogs. Some people keep drugs secreted in more private places, such as inside underwear, in places where secrecy is required. I once got busted in a London train station for just a small amount of marijuana in my pocket, when a sniffer dog leapt on me out of the blue. This sort of thing doesn't happen too often, but it's not what you want at all.

Apart from carrying drugs, the other thing to watch out for is your behaviour in public places, while under the effect of a drug. This seems obvious, and indeed you'll generally be fine as long as you can keep control of yourself and maintain awareness of your surroundings. However, some pretty outrageous public behaviour does occur as a result of drug use. I've witnessed some pretty stupid incidents, and been involved in more than a few idiotic episodes myself.

I've had to talk fast to persuade a nightclub bouncer not to eject my friend, after the friend in question gave an unsolicited, loved-up sweaty hug to the bouncer after one too many ecstasy pills. In the same nightclub, a friend and I had to think fast when another bouncer hammered angrily on the door while we were snorting drugs inside a toilet cubicle. Our solution was to exit and pretend that the reason the two of us had been in the same cubicle was that we were gay lovers. It worked pretty well; the beefy, macho bouncer was evidently discomfited by our camp, touchy-feely display, and let us off with a verbal warning.

# A COUPLE OF WAR STORIES

For a lot of people, drugs have had a big part to play in their formative experiences. It's not just the simple fact of taking drugs, of course – it's the people you meet and the absurd situations you get into. Certainly in my case, pretty much all of my repertoire of amusing anecdotes from my younger days involves getting twisted on one substance or another, and madness ensuing in some way. As I cast my mind back to try and recall the hazy details of those carefree, drug-addled times, different images come gradually into focus, of teenage shenanigans as well as later excesses.

A prime example is the time that a bunch of us took a big tent and a bag of ecstasy pills out to the woods, set the tent up on the top of a hill, and stayed there for the next three or four days, getting off our heads. Drugs pretty much replaced food and sleep, and the antics got progressively sillier. The interesting thing was that the pills we were getting throughout that summer, which went by the name of China Whites, had some kind of exotic trippy substance in them, alongside the ecstasy itself, that would kick in more during the comedown. You'd first spend a few hours all loved-up, chatty and huggy, then a bit later on your energy levels would fall a bit but your vision would really start playing tricks on you; things getting blurry, then distorted, and you'd even start seeing things that couldn't possibly be there.

I remember, at some point in the early hours, a group of us through the woods in the moonlight, and it really became like a dreamlike state. We started sharing hallucinations; one person would see something such as the lawn of a garden, and say to the others that we should be careful about where we were treading, and we'd all see the lawn with a small wall around it, but when we got there we found nothing but trees. At one point I found my friend talking intently with a tree, fully under the impression that he was having a conversation with somebody who was responding and replying to him. Another friend got lost in the dark and spent the next several hours alone in the woods; when he finally reappeared it became clear that he'd been five minutes away from our tent the whole time.

One situation where we used to take a lot of drugs was at free parties, also known as raves. This is where a sound system is set up either in an abandoned building or out in the countryside somewhere, and people gather, usually packed into cars in the case of the rural free parties, to dance, have fun and usually take some drugs. I've had some really great times at these parties, generally involving a lot of hugging and jabbering of nonsense at high volume and speed. Also, free parties have definitely yielded some good stories.

I remember one time there was a carload of us on the way to a free party. It was a full car and more; a pretty compact vehicle, with five people filling all the seats, as well as my friend Jack curled up in the boot because there wasn't space for him anywhere else. We had a couple of ounces of ganja, split up into small amounts for sale or trade at the party, and on top of this the driver, Tim, had been drinking before getting behind the wheel – not excessively, but he was definitely over the limit. Unfortunately, we'd only got about halfway to the party when we got pulled over by the police.

We were in a tight spot for sure, but we were saved by Tim's presence of mind. As the policemen got out of their car and came over, he quickly pulled out a two litre bottle of water from under his seat and downed as much of it as he could. This was commendable quick thinking under pressure, as sure enough the police demanded that Tim do a breathalyser test to check if he had been drinking. The large volume of water he'd drunk affected the result of the breathalyser, reducing the reading of his blood alcohol level so that it showed as being just on the boundary between legal and illegal. This meant that a second, more detailed test was required. We all sat there nervously, waiting for the results. If the police decided to search the car, they would find our weed, clearly divided into small portions for supply. If they opened the door of the boot, they would be greeted by the unhappy sight of Jack looking sheepishly back at them. As it was, Jack couldn't tell exactly what was going on from his position inside the boot, and kept knocking tentatively, only to be hissed at by the rest of us, telling him to shut up.

We sat in nervous silence for several minutes while the police processed the second breathalyser test. Then the policeman walked back over to the car and told us that Tim had passed this test, with a blood alcohol level just under the limit. They sneered at us to take care and drove off, and with a deep sigh of relief all round we continued our journey to the party. However, when we reached the party location we found that the police had closed it down and cordoned off the whole area. We drove off and found a quiet spot, let Jack out of the boot and smoked several joints, cursing the heavy-handed and officious police presence in our area.

I've hallucinated some crazy sights in my time, such as seeing the whole crowd at an outdoor music festival as zombies, complete with gore and missing body parts, which led to my stumbling and clawing my way to safety. I've lain giggling on my back as the clouds in the sky became surreal animated characters, moving at speed to wrestle and tumble over each other.

But, it has to be said, the truly memorable and important experiences that I look back on are not the ones where I was wasted.

# CONCLUSION

Well, you've made it all the way through my somewhat rambling, disjointed discourse on the weird world of drugs. Nicely done! Of course, what you have read is merely the point of view of one person, and my viewpoint is by no means authoritative.

What's for sure is that drug use can be great fun, and a conduit to some marvellous experiences. If you're lucky, you'll spend some precious time with some very special people, and pour out your most intimate thoughts and dreams in the middle of the night and know for certain that other people have the same things circling around in their minds. You'll see through the skin of reality that covers the world around us, and know that the life force that pulses through you is the same that sparkles through every living thing on the planet. You'll meet some entertaining idiots, and burble some incoherent nonsense with them in some unconventional surroundings.

Drugs have played a significant part in my personal development and growth, but they've also retarded both. To be perfectly honest, nowadays my memory is shot to pieces, I have a short attention span most of the time and I've wasted many, many opportunities that came my way through self-incapacitation with drugs.

When it comes to drugs, there's a difference between use and abuse. The line can be very hard to spot, and it's terrifyingly easy to slide from being someone who enjoys intoxication from time to time, to being someone who uses drugs as a crutch. You could easily wind up being psychologically or physically dependent on drugs, with your ability to deal with the real world being steadily reduced by the very substances you're using to escape from it. If you're going to use drugs, be careful and treat them with respect. You wouldn't want to end up like me.

CPSIA information can be obtained
at www.ICGtesting.com
Printed in the USA
LVOW12s1507171216
517722LV00001B/74/P